Weaving Your Thread In The Tapestry Of Judaism

Rob,

All the best.

Lev / Larry

Weaving Your Thread In The Tapestry Of Judaism

Lev Green

ISBN:	Softcover	978-1-4797-2767-4
	Ebook	978-1-4797-2768-1

Cover art: "By the rivers of Babylon . . . ," 2008
(detail of) woven tapestry by Berit Engen.

This book was printed in the United States of America.

To order additional copies of this book, contact:
Xlibris Corporation
1-888-795-4274
www.Xlibris.com
Orders@Xlibris.com
122219

Contents

To all those, past and
present, who have woven
their threads to create
this magnificent tapestry.

Preface

This manuscript is authored under my Hebrew name, Lev, meaning "heart" or "core". I do so because this work is written from my heart, and as a result of my love of Judaism. Judaism has become part of my core. My primary purpose in writing this book is to have Judaism become part of the core of those who have never been connected with our religion or who have become disconnected.

In every generation, Jews individually and collectively covenant with God as partners to be a shining example of righteousness for all of humanity, working toward a world free of violence and injustice. The tapestry of Judaism represents the interweaving of all of the individual threads of Jews past and present who have used their God-given talents toward this end. The tapestry continues to be woven, as we must do more to create this world. Each of us needs to weave our thread so that the tapestry may continue to be strong, so that the tapestry's brilliance may shine for all humankind.

Having provided the moral code for so much of humanity over the millennia, Judaism should be our moral compass as we lead our lives. For those who have never been connected with their Judaism, or who have lost their connection, Judaism offers so many portals through which you can become connected: synagogue, Torah study groups, havurah, music, brotherhood and sisterhood, meditation and Tikkun Olam. Indeed, there are people who have re-connected with Judaism through Jewish cooking classes. Once you enter through one of these portals, you begin to experience the richness of the gifts of Judaism, and you want to experience more.

Countless persons have contributed to my spiritual enrichment, and I would like to acknowledge some of them. I was greatly influenced by my Grandfather, Morris Berson (Z"L), with whom I had the privilege of joining at many a prayer service. I have been blessed with wonderful parents, David and Phyllis Green, who continue to set an example for all of us as a couple, as parents, as grandparents and now as great-grandparents.

I had a wonderful religious education at Temple Bethel in Great Neck, New York, and I wish to acknowledge Rabbi Jacob Rudin (Z"L) and Rabbi Jerome Davidson. I began my long-time affiliation with the American Jewish Society for Service as a 16-year old in 1968, devoting a summer to serving on a Northern Cheyenne reservation in Busby, Montana. Henry Kohn (Z"L), co-founder of AJSS, was a role model for me throughout much of my life, and I am honored to have succeeded him as Chair of this wonderful organization.

I have learned so much from my clergy over the years, through prayer services, Torah study and adult education, and I wish to acknowledge Rabbi Rifat Sonsino, Rabbi Emily Lipof, Rabbi Tom Alpert, Rabbi John Franken, Rabbi Sonia Saltzman and Cantor Randall Schloss.

Privileged to also be part of a longstanding lay led Torah study group, I wish to acknowledge Sharon Friedman, Marcia Szymanski, Brien Brothman, Sharon Parnes, Howard Tinberg, Toni Tinberg and Alan Wartenberg from that group.

My understanding and appreciation of Israel were enhanced as a result of a very meaninful and rewarding visit in February 2012. My wife and I are very grateful to Moshe, Tirza, Shachar and Yuval Hananel and to Ezra Bendori for all their generosity in conncetion with that trip.

I have certainly done a great deal of reading over the years, and there are four books that contributed significantly to this volume and which I recommend to all. "Faith Finding Meaning" by Byron

Sherwin is a wonderful treatise on the theology of Judaism, with emphasis upon our covenant with God. "The Ten Commandments in History" by Paul Grimley Kuntz is a very important work cataloguing the contribution of the Jewish moral code to Western Civilization. "The Death of Death" by Neil Gillman contributed to Chapter 7 of this volume. Finally, "The History of Love" by Nicole Krauss is an endearing novel with a wonderful subplot involving a boy who believes he is a Lamed Vavnik.

I am very appreciative to my assistant, Debra Giannotti, for her work in helping me with the preparation of this manuscript.

Finally, I want to thank my wonderful wife Ditzah (Denise) for all she has taught me, for creating a wonderful Jewish home, and for joining me in the richly intertwined Jewish life that we are privileged to live.

Introduction

Judaism has been described as a tapestry, a complex interweaving of individual threads, creating a most beautiful array of designs. The tapestry metaphor is most appropriate, given that the rich, brilliant fabric of Judaism has been at the center of human civilization over the past three millennia. The monotheistic tradition and teachings of Judaism have spawned Christianity and Islam, also Abrahamic religions practiced in one form or another by a majority of the inhabitants of our world. Setting forth a moral code defining human rights and responsibilities, Mosaic law has been at the heart of systems of law and justice for civilized societies over the centuries.

The tapestry of Judaism includes all of the stories of the Bible, the teachings of the Talmud and the wisdom of the Pirke Avot. The tapestry of Judaism has been colored by the entire history of our people, from God instructing Abraham Lech L'cha, to go forth, to our centuries of servitude in Egypt, to our years in the wilderness, to our flourishing in the Promised Land, to the destruction of the Temples, to the Diaspora, to the Spanish Inquisition, to the birth of the Chasidic movement, to the Holocaust, to the independence and development of the State of Israel.

The tapestry of Judaism includes an array of amazing designs in the form of beautiful and meaningful rituals, such as the lighting of Shabbat candles, the Kol Nidre chant, and the Passover Seder. The tapestry of Judaism is colored by our wonderful life cycle events, bringing families and communities together.

The tapestry of Judaism includes long and brilliant threads from individuals who have been at the forefront of every important field of human endeavor: science and medicine, philosophy and religion, literature and the arts, law and jurisprudence, government and economics. In each of these fields, Jews have been leaders throughout the centuries, with our collective imprint being grossly disproportionate to our numbers.

The tapestry of Judaism has been strengthened by the multitude of softer-color threads interwoven over the millennia by the millions of Jews who have quietly led their lives as righteous and honorable people and as good parents and teachers.

This volume is intended to encourage individual Jews, and especially those who are unconnected or have become disconnected with their Judaism, to understand that they have a role to play in contributing to the tapestry of Judaism. That tapestry has been so very important to the advancement of humankind. The tapestry continues to be woven, and it is critical that each of us weaves our thread.

Judaism should not be at the periphery of our lives. Instead, it should be a part of our core. Understanding Judaism's role in the world and our place in Judaism, each of us has the ability to contribute an important thread, thereby living a life of meaning and a life of significance.

Chapter 1

Resolving Doubts About God

God is at the center of Judaism. There is no Judaism without God. At the same time, doubt about God is a primary reason, if not the most significant reason, why Jews become disconnected from Judaism.

Doubt has been with us throughout Jewish history. In Parshah Beshalach in the Book of Exodus, one of the most dramatic of all Torah Parshiyot, Moses and the Israelites have fled Egypt following the last of the Ten Plagues, with God appearing as a pillar of cloud by day and a pillar of fire by night as the Egyptians are chasing the Israelites. God parts the Red Sea to permit the Israelites to pass through, enveloping the Red Sea around the chasing Egyptians. God springs water from rocks and provides manna from the heavens. And yet, even after all of these divine interventions and revelations, only a short time later, when the Israelites are thirsty and in search of more water, they ask, "Is the Eternal present among us or not?" Despite having witnessed the Ten Plagues and the parting of the Red Sea, the Israelites are doubting God's very existence.

In Parshah Beshalach, Amalek attacked the Israelites, and it is only with God's intervention that the Israelites are able to overcome Amalek. The Parshah concludes with the statement that there shall be a war by God against Amalek in every generation. Over the ensuing generations, Jewish Scholars identified Amalek as being any enemy of our people. Haman was said to be descended from Amalek. In more recent history, the Nazis and the PLO were identified with Amalek.

The Baal Shem Tov, the great Chasidic leader of the 18th century of the Common Era, taught that Amalek represented doubt about God, and that this was a great enemy that had to be overcome.

And indeed, doubt about God has been a continuing theme throughout our history, heightened during the most trying times for the Jewish people, including the destruction of the First and Second Temples, the Inquisition and the Holocaust.

And if our ancestors could have doubts even after witnessing the Ten Plagues and the parting of the Red Sea, then surely it is natural for Jews from all eras to have doubts, especially when they witness natural disasters and disease resulting in massive loss of innocent lives.

So how do we resolve our doubts? How can we reaffirm our belief in God? This is an essential issue, as God is at the center of Judaism.

What I would suggest to anyone in doubt are two propositions that are beyond refutation.

First, there was a creation. Yes, we can debate how the universe was created, but there can be no doubt that there was a creation, and that as a result of creation, we have so many gifts: the beauty of the universe, the natural resources of the Earth and the diversity of the many forms of life on Earth. And each of us has received individual gifts of our minds and our bodies, the ability to sense the wonder of the world in so many different ways, the ability to think, to reason, to imagine, to create.

When in doubt, think of God as gift, because each of these gifts is truly miraculous. We don't have to have a parting of the Red Sea to know and appreciate that there are gifts all around us, and as we experience these gifts, we are experiencing something majestic, and that is the majesty of God.

A second principle beyond any dispute: there is such a thing as good. We all know the power of good, and how different a world of good is from a world of evil. We should think of another of God's manifestations as the capacity for good.

God as gift and God as good.

The gift of creation is much bigger than any one of us, but it is also a part of who we are, as each of us has been given a gift with our body and our mind, and each of us has natural talents to be developed and shared with others.

And the concept of good is much bigger than any one of us, but again it is a part of who we are, as each of us has the ability to distinguish good from evil and to do good.

So God is everywhere, as the gift of creation is found everywhere, and the capacity to do good is everywhere. And God is also within us, as each of us is a product of creation and each of us has the capacity to do good.

Even if you should have doubt about the God who is all around us in the form of the gift of creation and the capacity for good, you can have no doubt about the divine spark that is within you, and you should look within as to how to best use your natural gifts to do good.

And to those who may still doubt, and who ask how can there be a God who would permit innocent people to die in natural disasters or in cancer wards, I offer this answer:

God as the gift of creation and the power to do good has afforded us all the tools we need to eradicate evil, sickness and justice. When people are dying in cancer wards, God wants us to use our gifts to aim higher and strive for more. We have brilliant doctors and scientists who find cures for disease, and in every generation there are greater advances, as we have dedicated parents and teachers who rear and train the next generation. And when innocent people are dying in fields of war, God wants us to aim higher and strive for more by working with one another toward peace with justice.

Prayer is our connection with God. If you have any doubt about the existence of a God that is omniscient and omnipotent, then you can still derive great meaning through prayer by looking to the divine spark that is within you, the gift of your body and your mind, your capacity to do good. Your prayer can be an act of true self-reflection as you consider how best to use your gifts and be a good and righteous person.

Chapter 2

Torah as a Living Document

The word "Torah" has been translated both as the "teaching" and the "law". Indeed, the Torah has been both an enduring teaching and a fundamental foundation of the law over the millennia.

The rule of law is what separates civilized society from anarchy and barbarianism. Absent the rule of law, it is the rule of force that prevails. The rule of force results in slavery and subjugation, rape and killing, and an overall deprivation of rights and a denial of the human potential. The rule of force and not the rule of law has prevailed during most of the history of humankind, and indeed, the rule of force and not the rule of law prevails in far too many places even in the 21st century of the Common Era. It is the rule of force that has resulted in genocide in Darfur. It is the rule of force that has permitted the Taliban to terrorize Afghans and to subjugate the entire female gender. It is only in societies where the rule of law prevails that rights are recognized and preserved, with force and might properly checked, and where humans can realize their dreams.

As Jews, we should take special pride in the very strong influence that our Torah has had in the overall evolution of the rule of law, and in particular in the moral basis of the law. Parshah Shoftim in the Book of Deuteronomy contains a number of passages regarding the rule of law. In Chapter 16, the Israelites are told to establish judges who shall judge righteously and that it is our obligation to pursue justice. Chapter 17 of Parshah Shoftim states that the King is not to be above the law, but instead the law is supreme. This is a very profound statement, preceding by two millennia a similar pronouncement in the Magna Carta. Written in 1215 of the Common Era, and espousing the supremacy of the law over the sovereign, the Magna Carta is recognized to be one of the most important documents in the history of civilized society, a forerunner of the American Declaration of Independence. And here he have in Shoftim the principle of the supremacy of the law over the sovereign two millennia prior to the Magna Carta.

The Magna Carta enunciated basic human rights, including the individual's right to life and liberty, rights which it recognized were bestowed by the Creator. Our Torah so provided two millennia earlier. In Parshah Re'Eh, God states "Behold, I have placed before you life and good, death and evil" and instructs us to choose life. And the Book of Exodus is of course a story about freedom, about our deliverance from slavery in Egypt, an affirmation of the God-given blessing of human liberty.

Our Torah addresses virtually every major area of jurisprudence, setting forth laws and codes addressing property rights, the enforcement of contracts, the relationship between master and servant, a system for crime and punishment, a listing of civil torts and recompense, a judicial system for judges, witnesses and the presentation of evidence. Indeed, thousands of years before anyone used the term "green laws", our Torah called for agricultural sabbaticals to protect the land.

Most significantly in the Torah is the codification of basic human morality in the Ten Commandments. In ten concise statements, we have an overarching moral code, defining how we are to lead our lives. After recognizing the oneness and holiness of God, the commandments tell us to remember the Sabbath Day and honor our fathers and mothers. There then follow the five commandments that are negatively worded, but in fact that affirmatively recognize important moral principles. The commandment not to murder recognizes the sanctity of every human life. The imperative not to commit adultery recognizes the sanctity of marriage. The commandment that we shall not steal recognizes basic property rights. The instruction not to bear false witness is a recognition of the principles of honesty and justice. And the commandment not to covet further reinforces the messages of the other commandments.

The moral code set forth in our Ten Commandments has been a basic foundation of the rule of law as it has been established throughout the civilized world, beginning with the Greek Empire. Philo Judaeus, a Jew living in Alexandria in the early first century of the Common Era, developed a synthesis of the morality of Mosaic law with the principles of rationality of Greek philosophy. The Ten Commandments were to eventually become part of the official religion of the Roman Empire. And Charlemagne, the most important of the Holy Roman Emperors, decreed that the Ten Commandments were to be a basic part of the study of all clergy, and to be preached and taught by the clergy to the public. Alfred the Great, King of the Saxons who lived in the 9th century, and whose kingdom included London, prefaced his code of Saxon law with the Ten Commandments.

The great political philosopher John Locke, whose writings were so instrumental in the evolution of democracy and in particular to the founding fathers of America, believed that the Ten Commandments were objective moral laws setting forth eternal and universal truths. Just as humans are capable, through their power of reason, of grasping mathematical truths, they are also capable of grasping the moral truths of the Ten Commandments. In other words, Locke viewed the Ten Commandments as being as axiomatic as basic mathematical truths.

Thomas Jefferson, the author of the Declaration of Independence, studied and understood the underlying morality that had evolved in the Judeo-Christian tradition. And in the first paragraph of the

Declaration we have the following sentence, that is part of the soul of every American and has also served as a model for those espousing the principles of liberty throughout the world: "We hold these truths to be self-evident, that all men are created equal, that they are endowed by their Creator with certain unalienable rights, that among these are life, liberty and the pursuit of happiness." This recognition that God has bestowed upon every human basic rights is a fundamental tenet of our Torah. The America Declaration of Independence has served and continues to be a model for free societies throughout our world.

Given its historical influence and its timeless lessons, we as Jews should truly appreciate the gift of Torah. Study of Torah should help us set our moral compass.

When we are called for an aliyah, we say in our prayer that God is giving us the Torah, not that God has given us the Torah in the past tense. The Torah is not an ancient document. Rather, it is a living document, from which new meaning can be derived every day.

When we recite the prayer for the study of Torah, we say that we are engaging in Torah, not simply reading Torah. This means that we immerse ourselves, our very souls, in Torah, deriving from the many lessons of each Parshah a better understanding of who we are, what are values should be and how we should live our lives.

When we read from and study Torah, we are instructed, as we are with any Jewish prayer, to look at and read the words, as opposed to simply reciting by memory or rote. That is because the Torah as a living document offers potential new insights with every reading. We live in dynamic and changing times, but the eternal lessons of the Torah are amazingly malleable, providing guidance as we encounter new situations.

Chapter 3

Our Covenant with God and the Concept of Chosenness

The relationship between God and the Jewish people is defined by the covenant, a sacred partnership. God promised to make the Israelites a great nation if the Israelites in turn followed God's law. Judaism teaches that the covenant was initiated by God as an act of love. Love is to be reciprocal, and in Deuteronomy Chapter 6, Verse 5, we are told to "love the Lord our God with all our heart, our soul and our might." The Torah is God's gift, and our Rabbis instruct that the gift of Torah at Mount Sinai was the equivalent of a ketubah, a marriage contract. A marriage entails not only love and passion, but also responsibility, and that is to follow God's commandments.

The covenant is not a concept that is in past tense. To the contrary, our Torah makes clear that the covenant is to be reaffirmed with God by every generation. That means that Jews in every generation, individually and collectively, are to reaffirm their love of God and also their responsibility moving forward. Indeed, Parshah Va'etchanan instructs us that if we keep our covenant and act with loving kindness, God will keep his commandments to a "thousand generations."

Our covenant with God is unique to us as the Jewish people:

"For you are a holy people to the Lord your God; the Lord your God has chosen you to be a people for His own possession out of all the peoples who are on the face of the Earth." Exodus 7:6.

In this and a number of other verses in the Torah, the Israelites are told by God that they are a chosen people. The Israelites are chosen because of God's love for them and because God keeps His covenant.

The concept of chosenness has been a troublesome concept for so many Jews over the centuries, and remains a troublesome concept for so many Jews today. Many Jews wish to avoid discussion of the concept altogether. Indeed, the concept of chosenness has been rejected altogether by Mordecai Kaplan, the founder of the Reconstructionist movement.

The misconception of so many about this concept is that chosenness somehow denotes some type of superiority, that Jews are somehow better than others or that we have a higher level of spirituality than others.

Nowhere in the Torah is there any sense that God has chosen the Israelites because they were superior to others. Any notion of superiority, let alone ethnic or racial superiority, is not only without merit but is understandably going to evoke an unfortunate reaction from others. And indeed, the improper connection between chosenness and superiority has unfortunately led to overreaction and anti-Semitism over the centuries.

At the same time, the concept of chosenness cannot be ignored or set aside, as it appears in a number of verses throughout the Torah. God made a covenant with Abraham, and reaffirmed the covenant with each of our patriarchs. God chose to give the Ten Commandments to our people. The Torah is replete with references that our people were chosen.

So instead of ignoring or rejecting the concept, we should embrace it, but we should do so with a sense of humility and a sense of responsibility.

We must be humble about the concept because chosenness does not mean superiority. And we should be further humbled because chosenness means that we have a responsibility to God and to humanity. The Prophet Isaiah referred to our responsibility to be a "light unto the nations". What this means is that we have received from God the Ten Commandments, a statement of the oneness of God and a moral code for how we are to live our lives. God gave our people the Ten Commandments not only to instruct us about the oneness of God and how to live our lives, but also to share with all humanity.

In our daily prayers, we thank God for making us Jews. God did choose us, and every day we should accept and embrace this concept with a sense of both humility and responsibility. If we lead our lives the way God has asked us to, being righteous people, positively touching lives and being a light unto the nations, we are fulfilling God's mission as a Chosen People.

Chapter 4

The People Israel and the Land of Israel

Israel is at the center of Judaism, both the people Israel and the Land of Israel. We are all a part of the people Israel, and we should all consider the Land of Israel as our homeland.

Notwithstanding enemy after enemy over the centuries, including those who were engaged in genocidal efforts, and notwithstanding our expulsion from our original homeland and from country after country in the Diaspora, the people Israel have not only survived, but indeed we have thrived. We did so because of the strength, richness and beauty of our multi-faceted religion. In numerous pockets spread throughout the vast Diaspora, our people held steadfast to their Judaism because of their faith in God, the teachings of Torah, the meaningfulness of our ritual, the power of our traditions. It is a remarkable history indeed.

The Bible makes reference to numerous societies that lived contemporaneously with the Israelites, and that were at least as numerous as the Israelites. These societies had their own theologies, based upon idolatry and polytheism. Yet we never hear again of the Philistines, Hittites, Moabites or Edomites. We and our tradition survived; theirs did not. Judaism survived not because our ancestors were stronger militarily, as they certainly were not. Instead Judaism survived, and indeed thrived, because of our acceptance of the oneness and greatness of God and the moral code and teachings of the Torah.

Each of us should take pride in this remarkable history. Each of us should be very proud to be part of the people Israel.

We take special pride in our forebears who resisted our enemies over the millennia: the Maccabees, the martyrs at Masada, the Marranos, the members of the Warsaw Ghetto. Our history continues to be written, and the Jewish people continue to have enemies. These enemies take many forms, including anti-Zionists and anti-Semites. Our enemies also take the form of the forces of assimilation. And our enemies take the form of our own doubt about our Judaism.

Especially in recognition of the countless who lost their lives in defense of our religion, each of us has a responsibility to be a meaningful part of the people Israel so that our religion can continue to survive and hopefully thrive. Judaism has played a crucial role in the advancement of civilization, but we have much more work to be done, and each of us must do our share.

In the Broadway staging of the wonderful and timeless musical "Fiddler on the Roof", Tevye and his family sing the "Sabbath Prayer" around their meager table in their small hovel. As the song progresses, we see other Jewish families, left, right and above, joining in the same prayers at their Shabbat tables. The image is so very powerful, because it demonstrates the strength of our numbers and also the strength of our oneness as a Jewish people. When we pray, we do so not only as individuals and as members of our Shuls, we also do so as part of the worldwide Jewish community.

Part of being a Jew is having an attachment to the Land of Israel. Jews are spread throughout the world, but one of the most important forces that should keep us together is the Land of Israel, as it is our common homeland. We should take great pride in what has been accomplished in the brief history of the State of Israel. Overcoming worldwide political and diplomatic resistance and having had to defend itself from military attack year after year, the State of Israel is nothing short of a miracle.

Taking full advantage of the natural resources of the land, converting desert and desolation into beautiful groves producing bountiful harvests, Israel has become a garden for the greater world, feeding its own people and exporting fruits and vegetables to Europe, Africa and Asia. Its citizens combining their diverse talents to work with one another to create and build thriving industries, Israelis are at the cutting edge of such important fields as computer software and biotechnology.

The Israeli government has made immense strides in preserving and restoring the multitude of historic venues throughout the land. The Land of Israel has been a critical crossroads throughout history. By virtue of the painstaking efforts of the Israeli government and its people, what has been preserved and restored is the history of a number of civilizations and societies. And with Jerusalem and a number of other cities and towns being holy cities for Christianity, Islam and Baha'i, the Israeli government and its people have demonstrated their respect for the millions of members of these faiths by preserving and protecting their churches, mosques and historic relics.

Israel has been a haven for the downtrodden and oppressed from all parts of the world. With a diverse population including peoples of a multitude of nationalities and religious backgrounds, living together largely in peace, we have in Israel a society that is closer than any other to the Messianic ideal.

Israel continues to face a host of enemies who are intent on wiping Israel out of existence. We must be supportive of Israel so that it may continue to be our homeland and a light to the entire world not only for our generation but for future generations.

Chapter 5

The Gift of Shabbat

We are commanded to observe Shabbat. The Ten Commandments make no mention of Rosh Hashanah or Yom Kippur, but we are commanded to observe Shabbat. Accordingly, Shabbat is an even more holy day than the High Holidays. God created the universe in six days, and on the seventh day, God rested. We are created in God's image, and we are also commanded to rest on the seventh day.

As Jews, we should observe Shabbat because it is a Commandment, but we should also appreciate Shabbat because it is a gift. With all the travails and distractions of our daily lives, we need a break. Yet Shabbat is not simply a day of rest, it is a day of self-reflection and spiritual sustenance. Through prayer, we reaffirm God's oneness and thank God for all our gifts. Through music, we augment the beauty and meaning of our prayers and we sense the strength of our community. Through study of Torah, we learn of our heritage and our moral code, with lessons to be learned as to how we should live our lives. Through silent prayer and meditation, we seek our own private communion with the God all around us and the divine spark within us.

With the gift of Shabbat, each of us has the opportunity to reflect back on the past week, to consider what we might have done differently, and each of us has the opportunity to look ahead to the coming week to resolve how we might do better.

Indeed, beyond reflecting on the past week and thinking ahead of the coming week, we should be considering more generally how we are living our lives, seeking spiritual guidance about how we can be a better spouse, a better parent, a better child and more righteous person.

Parshah Shemini is a beautiful parshah teaching about the building of a holy community. The entire community of Israelites, having been delivered from Egypt and having received the Ten Commandments, is now gathering for the first time around the newly constructed Mishkan, the Tabernacle. The Parshah is summed up in Leviticus Chapter 11, Verse 44: "You shall sanctify yourselves and be holy, because I am holy." God is holy. God has given the Ten Commandments to the Israelites and has asked that they become a holy people, as a model for the rest of the world. Another teaching of Parshah Shemini is that a holy community is constituted of holy individuals. When we think of what makes a person holy, we are not simply talking about how that person observes Shabbat. Instead, we are talking about how that person lives his/her life.

Judaism does not want us to be holy people just on Shabbat and secular people the rest of the week. Instead, we are to be righteous people in all that we do throughout everyday life, honoring our fathers and mothers, teaching our children, and treating all others with whom we interact with diginity and respect. As we pursue our livelihoods, we should not be divorced from principles of righteousness. To the contrary, principals of righteousness should guide all of our dealings with employees, employers, clients and customers.

Shabbat provides us the gift of rest and reflection so that we may obtain, through prayer and study of Torah, spiritual guidance and sustenance that will help us lead our lives as loving parents, spouses and children and as righteous people as we interact with others in our lives.

Chapter 6

Avodah

A cornerstone of Judaism is Avodah. The word "avodah" means labor, meaning anything requiring effort. But as capitalized, the concept Avodah means our acts and deeds in serving God. And as we serve God, we are partners with God in creation. The world is re-created everyday, and God has given us the resources to join in this re-creation and work toward a better world.

Deuteronomy Chapter 10 Verse 12 instructs that we are to labor for God with all our heart and our soul. How do we do this?

First, we have the opportunity to perform Avodah through mitzvahs, through good deeds. Mitzvahs come in all sizes and shapes, and we have the opportunity to perform mitzvahs everyday of our lives, visiting the sick, helping those in need, preserving our natural resources.

Tikkun Olam, repair of the world, is a central tenet of Judaism. Each of us possesses the gift of our minds and bodies, including our unique talents, to serve God by helping to repair the world.

God created a most beautiful world, but our world remains far from a perfect world. There is poverty, sickness and conflict throughout our world. Recognizing the principle of Tikkum Olam, we can work as God's partners to repair the world.

When we help others, we also reward ourselves. Studies have shown that people are at their happiest as a result of the gift of service to others. Through service, we derive a greater understanding of who we are and what is most meaningful in life.

We should not be discouraged by the enormity of the world's problems as we proceed with single acts of service. There is no act of service that is insignificant or meaningless. Every act of service has significance and meaning.

It is so very easy for anyone to look to a world where there is so much hatred and violence, disease and poverty, and to say that I cannot make a difference. The fact is you can. Indeed, Judaism teaches that when you save one life, you save the world.

We can also perform Avodah simply by being righteous people, by doing the right thing. Too often, individuals only do the right thing because others are looking. The truly righteous person also does the right thing when no one else is looking. The truly righteous person knows that all of our actions and omissions have consequences.

There is a concept in Judaism that at any point in time in history, there are 36 people on Earth who through their righteousness are responsible for saving humankind. These are the "Lamed Vavniks", as the Hebrew letters Lamed and Vav have a combined value of 36. We don't know who the Lamed Vavniks are, as they do their work without notice. Indeed, under one interpretation, Lamed Vavniks don't even know who they are, other then knowing that they are righteous people.

But here is a thought experiment: what would happen if each of us as individuals were to assume that he/she is a Lamed Vavnik? What a wonderful thought, because if each of us were to live our lives as truly righteous people, then surely the world would be a better place. And when all is said and done, that is what God expects of each of us, to be righteous and to set the example for all humankind.

Chapter 7

Our Time on Earth

"For you are dust and to dust you will return." Genesis 3:19

"There is a time for everything, and a season for even activities under the heavens: a time to be born and a time to die." Ecalesiastes 3:1-2.

We are all familiar with the Genesis story of Adam and Eve's disobedience of God by taking fruit from the Tree of Knowledge in the Garden of Eden. By this choice, they had the opportunity to achieve self-awareness and the power of discernment, but they were not to be immortal.

There has been a debate over the millennia as to the finality of death. While most of the Biblical passages on point speak to the finality of death, there are other passages suggesting that death is not final. Jewish thought was influenced during the Greek Empire, as the Greeks believed in the immortality of the soul. Jewish eschatological theory on the concept of death has taken a number of twists and turns over the years, with reincarnation and resurrection among the theories espoused at different times.

As frightening and unthinkable death may be, there can be no dispute that life is more meaningful because of death. This is especially so because none of us knows how and when we might die. Our days are numbered, and we don't know what the number is. We can live a ripe old age, or we could die well before our time. The certainty of death, combined with the uncertainty of the timing of death, provide additional meaning for our lives, because every day must count. We are all familiar with those who have recovered in remarkable fashion from a devastating sickness or a serious accident, and who attest to the fact that they view the world differently, making sure that they truly value each of their days.

While death may be final, each of us lives on after our death by the lives we touch. Indeed, we have the opportunity to touch lives of those who are born long after our death. Who can dispute that Moses Maimonides, Albert Einstein and Shalom Aleichem have touched countless lives of every generation following their deaths, and will continue to do so for generations to come?

We don't have to author great philosophic treatises, publish the general theory of relativity or write timeless literature to live on beyond our passing. We can do so be being good parents and grandparents, devoted teachers and mentors, and true friends and companions.

Humankind has conquered the three dimensions of space, as we have the ability to travel anywhere on Earth and indeed beyond. What we will never conquer is the fourth dimension of time. We cannot roll back time. What we can do is to make our time count. This is not to say that we must be doing something profound every second of the day. And certainly, rest and entertainment are part of who we are and part of what everyday life is and should include.

Yet we also know what wasting time is, and what lost opportunity is. And we know in a very poignant way that lost opportunities may be irreparable. When siblings have become estranged and fail to get back together before one passes away, that is an irreparable lost opportunity. When an individual wants to accomplish a task, but keeps procrastinating year after year, only to become physically or mentally impaired such that the task is never accomplished, that is an irreparable lost opportunity.

We should make every day of our lives count, and we should touch at least one other life in a positive and meaningful way every day of our lives.

Conclusion

Weaving Your Thread

As human beings, we seek meaning to our lives. We want to know why we are here on Earth and what our purpose is. Judaism provides us answers.

Our purpose is to join with God as partners in creation in working toward a Messianic Age, when violence and injustice have disappeared from the Earth, when people live together in peace. Judaism sets the example for the world, and each of us has the ability, an indeed the individual responsibility, to weave our thread in the tapestry of Judaism so that the example can be set.

In Parshah Va'etchanan, Moses pleads with God to permit him to enter the Promised Land. Moses had failed to obey God's instruction at Meribah, when the Israelites had complained of lack of water. God had instructed Moses to speak to a rock while the Israelites gathered around, and that water would then flow. Instead of following God's instruction, Moses proceeded to twice strike the rock. And while this resulted in water, God was unhappy with Moses because he had not trusted in God's word. God pronounced that Moses would die before entering the Promised Land. Given all that Moses did in assuming his leadership role, in confronting Pharaoh, in leading the Israelites out of Egypt and for forty years in the wilderness, for all that Moses did, he was to die before entering the Promised Land. And while

Moses must have been so very disappointed about this outcome, he must have also derived a sense of satisfaction about all that he had accomplished. Indeed, although God did not permit Moses to enter the Promised Land, God did permit Moses to climb to the precipice of the hill and to look out to the Promised Land. In looking out from the hill, Moses would have witnessed a beautiful land, and perhaps he also could foresee ahead to a Messianic Age.

Rabbi Tarfon, who lived in the period following the destruction of the Second Temple and whose wisdom is found as part of the Pirke Avot, pronounced: "You are not obliged to complete the work, but neither are you free to evade it." Moses was not able to complete his work, but he certainly did not evade it. Even after God's rejection of Moses' appeal to enter the Promised Land, Moses continued to teach and instruct the Israelites as to God's law, and Moses also provided instruction to his successor Joshua.

This is a lesson for all of us. Just as Moses never had the opportunity to enter the Promised Land, it is very likely that we will never see the Messianic Age, when violence and injustice have completely disappeared from the face of the Earth. Yet we are instructed by Rabbi Tarfon that while we are not obliged to complete the work, just because we won't see the completion does not mean that we should evade the work.

God has given us all the tools and resources we need to create a Messianic Age: our intelligence, our bodies, our diverse strengths and talents, the natural resources of the Earth. We have the resources to lift people from poverty and the intelligence to discover cures to diseases. And with God's gift of the Ten Commandments, forming an underlying basis for the legal systems of the civilized world, we have the ability to root out injustice. The tools are there, and it is up to us to use them correctly to work toward a Messianic Age.

Judaism instructs us that the world is re-created every day. With every new sunrise we have a new creation, with children entering our world, with new discoveries and inventions. Every day brings new possibilities, in the form of a cure to a disease or a new song or a new mode of communication.

If we live our lives in a righteous manner and use our God-given talents to try to improve the world, imparting these lessons to the next generation by being the best parents and teachers we can be, then we are weaving our thread, doing our part in working toward a Messianic Age. As Rabbi Tarfon also instructs: "The day is short, the labor vast, the toilers idle, the reward great, and the Master urgent." We may well not get there, just as Moses did not enter the Promised Land, but by doing our part and not evading the work, we should at least derive the satisfaction that we did our share in helping to achieve God's purpose.

About the Author:

Lev (Lawrence) Green is a practicing attorney and a student of Torah. Lev is the long-time Chair of the American Jewish Society for Service, a national non-profit organization that sponsors Jewish teens to perform Tikkun Olam in summer service projects. Now in its seventh decade, AJSS has sponsored over 2500 volunteers in service projects in 47 states, Canada and Israel. Lev is a graduate of Wesleyan University and New York University School of Law, where he was a Root-Tilden Scholar. Lev lives with his wife Denise in Brookline, Massachusetts, where they are long-serving members of Temple Ohabei Shalom. They have four grown sons and one grandson.

4811-1248-6160.1

CPSIA information can be obtained at www.ICGtesting.com
Printed in the USA
BVOW040347201112

305941BV00002B/5/P